KiDS!

200 Years of Childhood

Henry Francis du Pont Winterthur Museum
Winterthur, Delaware

Distributed by University Press of New England
Hanover, New Hampshire

Companion to the exhibition *KiDS! 200 Years of Childhood*, on display June 19, 1999, to February 19, 2001, Winterthur Museum, Garden & Library, Winterthur, Delaware.

This book reflects the hard work of many talented individuals:
Exhibition curator: Tracey Rae Beck
Text contributors: Tracey Rae Beck, Amber Auld Combs, Pauline Eversmann, Kimberly D. Meisten, and Beverly Serrell
KiDS! Activities contributors: Amber Auld Combs, Beth A. Twiss-Garrity, and Jennifer J. Hammond
Editor: Susan Randolph
Designer: Suzanne DeMott Gaadt, Gaadt Perspectives, LLC
Printer: West Lawn Communications

Photo credits: All photographs courtesy Winterthur except the following: page 12, Smithsonian Institution.

Library of Congress Cataloging-in-Publication Data

Kids! : 200 years of childhood.
  ISBN 0-912724-53-6
  1. Children--United States--History Exhibitions. I. Henry Francis du Pont Winterthur Museum.
HQ792.U5K49 1999
305.23'074751'1--dc21   99-26146
                                                                     CIP

TABLE OF CONTENTS

Special Section
KiDS! Activities

WHAT IS CHILDHOOD?

Childhood. Think about the meanings that this word has for us today. We think of childhood as a time to grow, a time to play, a time to learn, a time to protect, a time of risk, a time of exploration—the worst time, the best time.

Did childhood evoke the same meanings for people in America in the eighteenth and nineteenth centuries? Did adults wistfully remember their childhood as a magical time and try to duplicate it for their children? Or, did parents remember their childhood as a difficult time and seek to improve their children's experiences? Indeed, was there even such a concept as childhood, or is it a twentieth-century invention that we now assume has always existed?

These are not easy questions to answer, in part because there can be no one, universal concept of childhood. How past generations viewed childhood depended on many factors, including where individuals grew up, their parents' occupations, and their legal status as free, indentured, or enslaved Americans. A child working on a farm in New England, the daughter of wealthy Philadelphians enrolled at needlework school, or an

WALKING STOOL

New England; possibly late 1700s

Society for the Preservation of New England Antiquities

People today might find it difficult to identify this object. Known in the 1700s as a walking stool or go-cart, the wooden frame supported babies as they took their first hesitant steps. Unlike modern walkers, a walking stool did not have a seat to support the infants when they grew tired of standing on weak, unsteady legs. Parents viewed early walking as important because it helped a child to leave behind infancy, which parents perceived as a dangerous time. The stool also discouraged a child from crawling, an activity that some adults considered animalistic.

enslaved African girl serving as a housemaid in Virginia—all experienced childhood very differently. The time period under consideration also plays an important role. Parents in the early 1700s held very different views of childhood from those at the end of the century, and their views, in turn, differed from those of adults living in the mid-1800s.

How, then, can we tell the story of two hundred years of childhood in America? Where do we go to find out what childhood meant to parents and to children at different times in history? We start with objects, with the tangible remains of past lives. We look at those items that have survived and ask questions about what they meant to people living long ago. We turn to books, to diaries, to letters, and to other written evidence, all of which serve as important resources that tell us what people considered important enough to record and preserve. We also look for what has not survived and try to figure out why.

Yet, one question remains: Why do we want to learn about childhood in the eighteenth and nineteenth centuries at all? Does it matter to us today what people in past times thought about children's lives or what children in the past thought about their own lives? The answer is "yes" because history offers perspective and hindsight. Learning from the past allows us to think about the present and to put current issues into perspective.

History also puts us in touch with ourselves. Think about how many times we have listened to our parents or grandparents talk about what life was like when they were young. We marvel when they talk about typing a term paper on a manual typewriter or describe using carbon paper to make copies. We try to imagine what it must have been like to crawl out of bed on a cold winter morning to shovel coal into a furnace or to throw more logs into a wood-burning stove. We smile in disbelief when they speak of walking many miles to school in the bitter cold or freezing rain. We are sobered when they discuss the Great Depression or their experiences in wartime. We listen to and enjoy these stories because they connect us with our personal heritage.

The exhibition *KiDS! 200 Years of Childhood* explores the many and varied ways in which parents shaped the world of children in America between 1700 and 1900. It looks closely at the furniture, books, clothes, toys, and games used by children, and it tells stories about growing up in early America. Above all, it invites us to learn through history, demonstrating how historical objects and stories not only put us in touch with the past but also move us closer to understanding the present.

CHILDREN IN THE HOME

All children (past and present) need shelter, clothing, and food in order to grow and thrive. Although these basic needs have not changed over time, how adults have defined and met these needs has changed.

An Adult's World

In the 1600s and early 1700s, most parents did not think of childhood as a distinct phase of development. Instead, they expected children to become part of the adult world swiftly. Because many babies died during infancy, adults considered it a dangerous time, and they encouraged children to move rapidly from the dependency and vulnerability of infancy to the self-sufficiency and stability of adulthood.

During the first half of the eighteenth century, few objects existed that were made especially for children, and those that did were often used to hasten the transition from infancy to adulthood. Parents employed such items as walking stools, narrow cradles, and tiny corsets to straighten and strengthen young limbs and to encourage children to walk as quickly as

WINDSOR CRADLE

United States; 1775–1825

64.1524 Winterthur Museum, bequest of Henry Francis du Pont

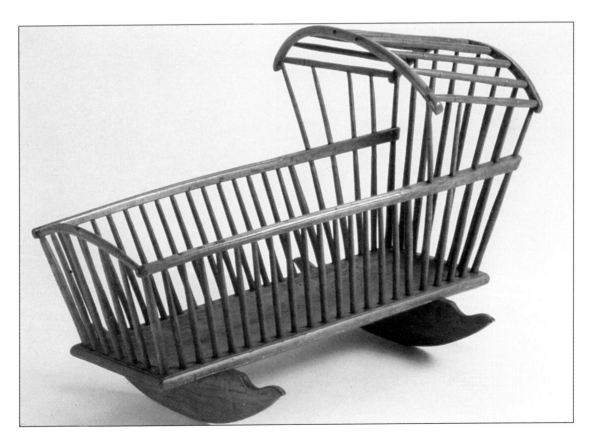

CRIB

United States; 1770

78.90 Gift of
Mrs. James M. Castle

Only the wealthiest child enjoyed a toy rattle like the silver and coral one shown here in a crib. Fashioned by preeminent Philadelphia silversmith Joseph Richardson Sr., the tiny bells on this rattle amused the baby while the coral helped the child teethe. The infant could chew on the elegant plaything to relieve the pain of sore gums. In addition to serving as a teething aid, coral was believed by some to protect children from disease and evil, an important quality since many parents viewed teething as potentially dangerous to a child's health.

CHILD'S RATTLE (in cradle)

Made by Joseph Richardson, Sr.

Philadelphia, Pennsylvania; 1734–50

56.560 Winterthur Museum, gift of Henry Francis du Pont

possible. Adults also swaddled infants (wrapping them tightly in strips of cloth that kept them immobile) in an effort to help them develop straight, strong bodies and prepare them for early walking.

From a very early age, children in colonial America dressed like adults. When they grew too old to be swaddled, boys and girls both wore dresses, also called "long coats," that extended several inches below their feet and prevented them from crawling, a practice some adults considered animalistic. Once children could walk, their dresses (which resembled their mothers' apparel) only fell to the ankles. When boys reached six or seven years of age, they were "breeched," or put into trousers like their fathers wore. Girls continued to wear dresses like their mothers'.

The absence of toys made specifically for children during this period further reinforces the notion that childhood was not seen as a distinct phase of life at this time. The few surviving amusements from the colonial era, such as playing cards and

THE GORE CHILDREN

Made by John Singleton Copley

Boston, Massachusetts; 1753

59.3408 Winterthur Museum, gift of Henry Francis du Pont

John Singleton Copley, one of America's best-known artists, painted this portrait when he was only fifteen. Copley posed the children in the stiff and formal manner considered proper for portraiture at the time. Notice how the children are dressed: the three older children—a brother and two sisters—wear clothing that resembles adult apparel. The youngest child, a boy, wears a dress, indicating that he is not yet old enough to wear breeches.

tops, as well as written evidence about early recreation, indicate that children and adults shared both playtime and playthings. An examination of floor plans from houses of the late 1600s and early 1700s strengthens the observation. The most common plan indicates only two rooms within a household: the downstairs hall and the upstairs chamber. All of the family's daily activities, including cooking, eating, working, playing, and sometimes sleeping, took place in the hall. The upstairs chamber served as the family's sleeping quarters, where children shared beds with adult family members.

A Shared World

By the mid-1700s, the acceptance of an influential philosophical movement called the Enlightenment heralded a change in prevailing ideas about childhood. Parents began to recognize childhood as an important and natural stage of human development. Instead of encouraging their children to walk and become independent as quickly as possible, they began to appreciate childhood as an ideal time to educate children and influence their moral growth.

The appearance of adult furniture forms sized especially for children, such as small chairs and stools, document this changing attitude. Windsor furniture, especially popular because the open, airy design was considered particularly healthful, became a preferred style for the increasing variety of children's furnishings, which included child-size tables, beds, and benches.

As the variety of child-focused goods expanded, so too did the sizes of homes in America. The larger houses often included a back parlor or sitting room that functioned as a family gathering place. Here, in a room distinct from the kitchen or formal front parlor, the family ate, read, sewed, played, and relaxed together.

Believing that children were naturally fit and strong, parents made little effort to protect children from the cold. Boys and girls wore short-sleeved clothing made from lightweight fabric year-round. Boys often wore one-piece outfits called "skeleton" suits, or jumpsuits, that served as a transitional form of attire worn after boys outgrew the dresses of their infancy and before they adopted men's breeches. Girls continued to wear lightweight dresses with high waists similar to their mothers' clothing. Swaddling also fell out of favor during this period as it was thought to restrict a child's natural development.

Parents now recognized play not only as a healthful activity but also as an educational opportunity. Toys became an integral part of a child's physical development. Some toys reinforced gender roles and prepared children for their future responsibilities as men and women. Playing with toy farm animals, for

example, helped prepare a boy for the day when he might assume control of the family farm. Other playthings promoted the development of universal skills, such as improved hand-eye coordination or dexterity. A proliferation of books written especially for children also made playtime educational, encouraging young boys and girls to improve reading skills.

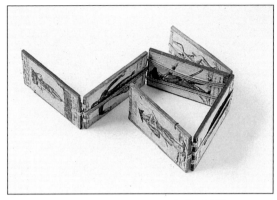

JACOB'S LADDER

Germany or Pennsylvania; 1790–1820

55.50.11 Winterthur Museum

Playing with a Jacob's ladder required a certain amount of dexterity. The trick to making the ladder move properly lies in a deft wrist action. The name for the toy comes from the biblical story of Jacob, who saw in his dream a ladder leading to heaven.

A World Apart

In the early 1800s, the perception of childhood as a natural stage of development was replaced by a romanticized notion of childhood as an age of innocence and purity. Popular writers portrayed children as angelic creatures who descended directly from heaven. The adult world into which children were easily integrated in the 1700s now assumed a more menacing appearance. Parents believed that children, as unspoiled beings, needed to be protected from the corrupting influences of this adult environment.

Thus, by the mid- to late 1800s, growing up was seen as a process of degradation rather than as a progression in life. Parents sought to prolong the period of childhood and to protect a child's innocence. An effective way to perpetuate a state of innocence was to keep children isolated from the adult world, so Victorian parents provided children with their own room—the nursery—and purchased specific furniture forms that further separated children from adult experiences. There, isolated from the evil influences of the outside world, children slept, played, and often ate.

In addition to shielding children within the protected environment of the nursery, adults began to acquire distinctly child-focused objects. High chairs, baby buggies, and baby jumpers all served to contain and separate children from the adult world. A high chair provided a barrier between children and the dinner table, thereby allowing children to be a part of the adult dining experience while according them their own space. Another newly adopted children's furniture form, the baby carriage, became popular because it not only enabled infants to experience the healthful benefits of fresh air but also allowed them to be safely displayed in public. A baby jumper, similar to a modern swing, not only kept a child out of harm's way but also protected adult belongings from children's curious fingers.

During this period changes in clothing customs further emphasized the separation of children from the world of adults. Between the ages of three and seven, both boys and girls wore short dresses with pantaloons. This form of dress provided ample freedom of movement for play and prolonged a child's happy ignorance of gender differences. Although a controversial practice, young women also began wearing pantaloons, allowing them to ride bicycles and otherwise engage freely in outdoor activities while providing a necessary measure of modesty.

By the late 1800s, the increasing industrialization of the United States coincided with a new attitude toward play, which parents began to view as a principally recreational activity. Mass-produced toys became more affordable, and more children had dolls, hoops, games, and other small toys with which to amuse themselves.

BABY JUMPER

Made by Glascock Brothers Manufacturing Company

Muncie, Indiana; 1892–1907

National Museum of American History, Smithsonian Institution

This object resembles the modern baby swing and, indeed, served much the same purpose in the 1800s. Made for use by children up to age six, the baby jumper allowed a child to be rocked back and forth by an adult or to use his or her own body weight to bounce up and down. More important for nineteenth-century parents, it also isolated and protected a child from the adult environment.

Children in the Home

From the early days of settlement in America to the end of the nineteenth century, how adults and children defined and shared domestic spaces within the home changed in important ways. While parents and children in the 1700s often lived and played together in the same room, by the early 1800s, they frequently gathered for dining and comradery in a shared common room but played and slept separately. Following the introduction of the nursery around 1850, children frequently slept, ate, and played in this protected space, isolated from the adult world and its corrupting influences. They interacted with their parents only under controlled circumstances. Thus, although the amount and type of interaction between parent and child changed over time, the idea of home as a place for parents to nurture and teach their children has remained constant to the present.

A CHILD'S DRESS

United States; 1860–80

94.107.3 Winterthur Museum, gift of Eleanor A. Murphey in memory of Henry H. and Maria M. Albertson

This child's dress might have been owned by either a boy or a girl. Through unisex clothing, parents sought to protect the innocence of children by delaying their recognition of gender differences.

TABLE CROQUET

United States; 1880–1900

69.2193a-ii Winterthur Museum, bequest of Henry Francis du Pont

Table croquet provided members of a Victorian family (young and old alike) with an opportunity to play together. The game consists of a green cloth that would have been spread over a table. Miniature mallets, balls, and striped posts constituted the necessary equipment for playing the game. A decorated belt around the edge of the cloth defined the boundaries of play. With this game, a family might pass a rainy afternoon by enjoying a pleasant game of indoor croquet.

LEARNING FOR LIFE

Just as the home environment created by parents for their children changed over time, so too did the methods and materials used to educate children.

Learning to Be Good

Today, as in the past, parents regard the development of a strong moral code in children as one of the most important responsibilities of raising a child. In the 1700s, religion heavily influenced a child's education. The prevailing religious belief in the colonies during this period emphasized that children were born into this world with the stain of sin and depravity already stamped upon them. Although parents believed it was their job to help children conquer their sinful natures, the ultimate responsibility for moral behavior rested with the child. Therefore, adults tried to instill in children a respect for divine authority by encouraging them to pray, by taking them to church, and by enforcing strict discipline.

Many parents baptized their children within a few days of birth. The baptismal ceremony was important because it not

THE NEW GAME OF VIRTUE REWARDED AND VICE PUNISHED

By William Darton

London, England; 1818

74 x 438.201 Winterthur Library

This nineteenth-century board game is similar to the modern game Chutes and Ladders. Players tried to "do good" and land on "Virtue" in the center of the game to win the accumulated bank of play money.

*"TAUF-WUNSCH," A BAP-
TISMAL GREETING (Fraktur)*

*Attributed to the Sussel-
Washington Artist*

*Berks County, Pennsylvania;
1771*

*58.120.15a Winterthur
Museum, funds for pur-
chase provided by Henry
Francis du Pont*

Pennsylvania Germans cre-
ated beautiful documents
called Fraktur (which
means "broken writing")
to commemorate special
events, such as marriages,
baptisms, and confirma-
tions. The custom of cre-
ating a document to cele-
brate a baptism dates to
the 1500s, when an
infant's godparents would
present the newborn with
a gift of coins wrapped in
paper. This Fraktur, given
at the baptism of Stovel
(Christopher) Ehmrich,
lists his sponsors, or godparents.

only absolved children of original sin but also welcomed them
into the family's religious community. While baptism set
Christian children on the road to salvation, the rite of circumci-
sion represented a Jewish boy's covenant with God and his
membership within the world of Judaism. From birth, children
were accountable members of their particular religious community, and as such they were taught to be good neighbors within
a congregation.

Those children who survived infancy were not shielded
from the notion of death. On the contrary, parents used every
opportunity to remind children that the way they behaved in
life would have eternal consequences. Facing death joyfully was
considered a virtue, and many children's stories reinforced this
lesson. The book *A Token for Children, Being an Exact Account of
the Conversion, Holy, and Exemplary Lives, and Joyful Deaths of
Several Young Children*, for example, contained tales of children
who had converted to Christianity when they were as young as
two or three and who died bravely.

Good manners distinguished a well-raised child from
one whose moral instruction had been neglected. Parents spent
considerable time teaching and reinforcing good manners, but
not all lessons were presented in serious
tones. While some etiquette books somberly
declared that poorly behaved children would
bring disgrace to their parents as well as to
themselves, other books featured colorful pictures and amusing rhymes that taught the
same lessons in a more playful manner. In
The School of Good Manners, written by Nancy
Sprout and published in 1822, humorous car-
toons discouraged improper behavior, such as
blowing one's nose in public.

OUR FAMILIES, OURSELVES

Using information from this book and from the exhibition *KiDS! 200 Years of Childhood*, think about how we live today and how children and parents lived in the past. Do we have more or less things for children in our houses? How do today's schools differ from those of the past? Do we enjoy the same toys and games as people did in the past? Discover for yourself.

◀ Look at how these sisters and brothers from long ago dressed to have their portrait painted. Can you tell which are boys and which are girls? How do you dress for school pictures or family photographs?

Find a photo of you with your family and place it in the frame. Or draw a family portrait with markers or crayons.

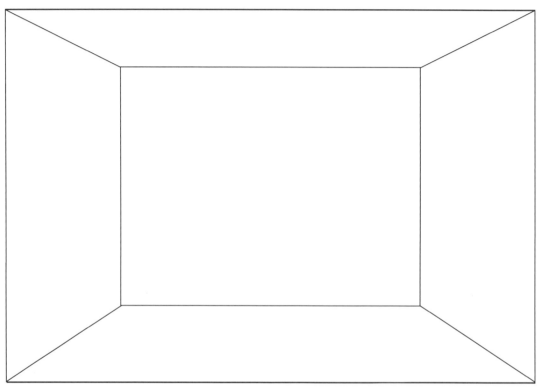

Just as families today look different from those in the past, families today live differently than they did long ago. In the early 1700s, children and adults usually lived together in one room called the hall. Families would cook, eat, and even sleep in this one room. Most objects in the house were intended for adults. Children used the same furniture as adults and even played the same games.

Think of the room in your home where your family spends the most time together. Write the name of that room on the dotted line above and then draw a picture of everything you see in that room. Using different colors, show which things are used by children, which things are used by adults, and which things are shared by both.

This child, _____ ,

first glanced at the light of the world in the state of

_____ ,

and created this Fraktur to remember visiting

Winterthur Museum on _____ .

Just as we do today, people in the 1700s and 1800s marked important moments or achievements in their children's lives with special remembrances. German families often celebrated with fancy certificates called Fraktur. The artist would write the occasion being celebrated and decorate the Fraktur with birds, tulips, hearts, and other brightly colored designs (see the example shown on page 16).

Here is a Fraktur to celebrate your visit to Winterthur.
Fill in the blanks and decorate it with your own design.

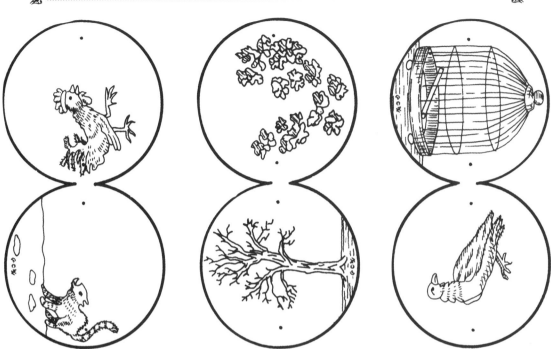

Toys for Fun in the Blink of an Eye

People in the 1800s played with toys that tricked their eyes into seeing a wonderful world of dancing drawings. Follow the directions below to make these optical toys called thaumatropes, and you won't believe your eyes.

Directions for Making Thaumatropes

1. Color the pictures in the circles.

2. Cut out each pair of circles, leaving them joined in the center.

3. Fold each pair of circles in the center, back to back. Glue or tape each pair of circles together.

4. Insert a piece of string 8 inches long with a knot at one end through the dots at either side of the circles.

5. Hold the strings, one in each hand, and roll the strings between your thumbs and forefingers. The back-to-back pictures will look like one image.

Thaumatrope designs adapted by Grace Patterson from documents in the Downs Collection, Winterthur Library.

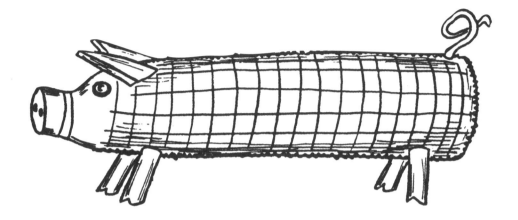

Making Toys That Are Simply Fun

People in the past used everyday items to make toys for their children.
Try making the toy shown above, and see for yourself
how much fun toys made from ordinary objects can be.

Corncob Pig

1. Take a corncob, and trim the stem end to make a snout.

2. Cut four holes at the bottom of the corncob for the legs and two holes at the top of corncob for the ears. If you'd like, you can cut holes for the eyes and nose too.

3. Roll up small pieces of cornstalk and glue them into the holes to make the legs and ears. Shape the ears and feet to give your pig just the right look.

Corncob pig adapted from Dick Schnacke, *American Folk Toys: How to Make Them*
(New York: Penguin Books, 1973), pp. 94–95.

Games for Thought

In the past, children played games that educated as well as entertained. The games below come from a book in the Winterthur Library that describes pastimes for children in the early 1800s. Play these games to discover how learning the ABCs and solving math problems can be all fun and games.

Alphabetical Compliments

While you take turns saying the letters of the alphabet, before each letter, say "I like you because . . ." and then add a compliment beginning with your letter. For example, "I like you because you are Awesome"; "I like you because you are Beautiful"; "I like you because you are Careful"; and so on. If you skip a letter or can't think of a compliment beginning with that letter, you are out of the game.

Magic Arithmetic

Tell someone to think of an even number from 1 to 10 but not to tell you the number. Ask the person to double the number and then tell them an even number to add to it. Tell the person to cut the new number in half and then subtract the original number from it. Now you tell them that the number that remains was their secret number. The trick is that the final number always will be half of the even number you told them to add. For example, if you told them to add 4, the answer will be 2.

A Blast from the Past

Try playing some of these games that were enjoyed by children in the past and remain popular today.

Marbles
Bicycle Riding

Jumping Rope
Blowing Soap Bubbles

Hide-and-Seek

Games adapted from Lydia Maria Child, *The Girl's Own Book*
(New York: Clark Austin and Co., 1833), pp. 20, 185–86.

Someday people will write about what it was like to be a kid in the 1990s. How can you make sure they get it right?

Make a time capsule! Think about what a museum in the year 2100 should display to explain what it was like to be a kid in 1999 or 2000.

1. **Find a container.** Remember, it has to last for a hundred years and keep out bugs, water, or other potentially damaging elements. Some people use metal boxes or plastic storage containers.

2. **Decide what to put in it.** Your report card? A popular toy? Your sneakers? Think about what you wish you knew about how kids lived long ago. Do you want to know what games they played or what they liked to eat? Put something in your capsule that will answer those questions about you for your great-grandchildren.

3. **Put your time capsule somewhere safe** where your family can find it a hundred years from now.

Be a detective! Find out what it was like to be a child when your parents or grandparents were young.

1. **Find a time when you can talk to your family** or friends about what their life was like when they were kids. A family party or holiday is a good time, or maybe you can plan a special visit.

2. **Get people talking.** Old pictures or objects that have been passed down through the family may help bring back memories. It also helps to ask a few questions, such as "What did you do in school?"

3. **Record what you learn.** Have a tape recorder or video camera running to tape what the person says.

Suggestions for Further Reading

If you'd like to learn more about—

. . . being a kid long ago, read:

Kate Waters, *Samuel Eaton's Day: A Day in the Life of a Pilgrim Boy*. New York: Scholastic Inc., 1993.

Kate Waters, *Sarah Morton's Day*. New York: Scholastic Inc., 1989.

Ann McGovern, *If You Lived in Colonial Times*. New York: Scholastic Inc., 1964.

Deborah Roberts Kerk, *A Day in June*. Sturbridge, Conn.: Old Sturbridge Village, 1982.

. . . how kids learned long ago, read:

Judith Hoffman Corwin, *Colonial American Crafts: The School*. New York: Franklin Watts, 1989.

. . . toys and games, read:

Bobbie Kalman, *Historic Communities: Colonial Life*. New York: Crabtree Publishing Co., 1992.

Henry Bursill, *More Hand Shadows to Be Thrown upon the Wall*. New York: Dover Publications, 1971.

David C. King. *Colonial Days: Discovering the Past with Fun Projects, Games, Activities, and Recipes*. New York: John Wiley and Sons, 1998.

. . . how to preserve your family's history, read:

David Weitzman, *My Backyard History Book*. Boston: Little, Brown, 1975.

Ira Wolfman, *Do People Form on Family Trees?* New York: Workman Publishing, 1991.

Parents in both the 1700s and 1800s took advantage of every opportunity to impress upon children the importance of leading a good life. Even playtime served as an educational opportunity, and objects such as jigsaw puzzles, board games, and picture books all stressed the need for good behavior and the consequences of bad conduct.

Parents and teachers also realized the importance of rewarding good behavior in the classroom. Tokens such as mugs, medals, and merit cards—adorned with pretty pictures, sayings, and Bible verses—rewarded deserving children and served as incentives for disobedient youngsters. Mark Twain used the Sunday school merit card system to great advantage in his *Adventures of Tom Sawyer*. Young Tom, who stubbornly resisted all attempts at moral improvement, skillfully traded "lickrish and fish-hooks" (gained during his infamous fence-painting scheme) for merit cards in order to qualify for the grand prize, a Bible. The astonishment of his Sunday school teacher was great indeed.

Places of Learning

Few children attended school in the 1700s. Rather, they learned life skills, as well as reading, writing, and arithmetic, at home. Mothers, fathers, and older brothers and sis-

Teaching children to behave properly in public was of upmost importance to parents in the 1700s and 1800s. *The School of Good Manners: Composed for the Help of Parents in Teaching Their Children How to Behave in Their Minority* included such advice to children as "spit not, cough not, nor blow thy nose at the table, if it may be avoided. But if there be necessity, do it aside, and without much noise."

UNCUT HANDKERCHIEF

United States; 1850–1900

80.70 Winterthur Museum, gift of Mr. and Mrs. Lammot du Pont Copeland

Along with the growing concern for children's education during the 1800s came an increasing number of teaching aids. Printed handkerchiefs, such as the one shown here, helped schoolmasters teach children reading, writing, and arithmetic. Notice the school scenes that adorn this cloth.

ters often served as their teachers. By the 1800s, however, common (or public) schools and Sunday schools became focal points of more organized educational efforts.

Sunday schools (also known as Sabbath schools) emerged in the 1790s, primarily to educate children whose parents could not or would not teach them at home. The schools taught reading, writing, and arithmetic and further shaped juvenile behavior by preventing children who worked during the week from becoming disruptive on Sundays. By the 1820s, Sunday schools in America served children of all economic classes, and curriculum began to emphasize moral and spiritual lessons.

Common schools began to be developed in the 1820s as a way to provide a proper and free education for all children—an education that would prepare virtuous citizens to participate in an enlightened, democratic society. The common school movement promoted the adoption of a standardized curriculum, which included science and music, as well as new teaching methods and specialized children's furniture forms for greater classroom organization.

Common school advocates enthusiastically embraced and promoted its ideals, but the movement fell short of its goals. Rural areas with sparse populations could not support school systems,

ELLEN; OR, THE NAUGHTY
GIRL RECLAIMED

Published by S. and J.
Fuller

London, England; 1811

Col. 121 74 x 438.25
Downs Collection,
Winterthur Library

To urge girls to "cultivate kindly feelings," this book and paper doll set taught that a stubborn, naughty child could potentially lose the love and support of her family and friends. Ellen's descent from a spoiled, willful child into lonely poverty and her subsequent redemption are traced through costume changes. For each stage of Ellen's journey, the reader is given a paper dress to put on the figure of Ellen.

and the demands of farming frequently required that children work at home to support their family rather than attend school. Thus, rural schools suffered in comparison to those in urban areas. In addition, racial, religious, and economic differences made it difficult to provide a balanced curriculum and equal education to all students.

Learning the Three R's

From the earliest times, reading was the most important and the first skill taught to children in America. The importance attached to reading originated with the Puritans, who believed everyone should be able to read the Bible. Despite the emergence of schools and the emphasis placed on reading, however, in the 1700s, almost half of the children in America could not read because they were enslaved or indentured to masters who did not honor the terms of their apprenticeship contracts.

For those children who *were* taught to read in the 1700s, the Bible, prayers, and religious stories served as the most common textbooks in the home. Beginning in the 1800s, however, reading materials began to focus on history and stressed the value of being a good citizen. In addition, books were increasingly designed with children in mind. Features such as large print, colorful pictures, and short chapters engaged a child and made learning fun.

Although most children learned to sign their names, prior to the 1750s, writing was primarily an upper-class skill. In schools, children learned to write between the ages of eight and ten. The most common teaching method involved copybooks, in which a child practiced writing skills by copying the same sentence over and over. In so doing, children not only improved their penmanship but also learned the values described in the sentences. Young Elizabeth Taylor, for example, repeatedly inscribed the saying "Quit thyself nobly, with a prudent care/Of clumsey Writing and of Blots beware" in her copybook in 1785. This method survived well into the twentieth century.

The least emphasized of the three R's, arithmetic was taught to children in the 1700s with practical applications in mind, such as how to maintain household records or convert prices to different currencies. Younger children may have received rudimentary instruction in "ciphering," as it was called, but the more sophisticated instruction was reserved for older children who planned to enter a trade and become a surveyor, architect, shopkeeper, navigator, or teacher. As in reading, teachers recognized the need to engage a child's imagination and sense of play in the learning process. Tools to teach math

THE DIGITS IN THE FIGITS, CONSISTING OF COMICAL POSTURES AND CURIOUS EXPLANATIONS

England; 1750–1800

60.174 Winterthur Museum

Even the most disinterested math student could enjoy learning numbers from this print. Each "figit" forms a number and is accompanied by a didactic verse, such as "He's a SIX here complete, with his Hands to his Feet."

The DIGITS in the FIDGETS, consisting of COMICAL POSTURES and CURIOUS EXPLANATIONS.

included the abacus, humorous prints, and games.

A basic knowledge of math was necessary for anyone who would engage in commerce, whether as a shopkeeper or a farmer. Because the value of American money was not standardized until after the 1820s, knowing how to figure sums in British pounds sterling or how to determine the relative value of others states' currencies were vital skills.

Learning to Work

Along with teaching moral values and the three R's, parents recognized the importance of developing a strong work ethic in their children. From 1700 to 1900, work occupied the major portion of a child's day. The amount, as well as the type, of work performed by children depended on several factors: where they lived, their gender, the size of their family, their economic status, and, in many cases, the season of the year.

Children's chores typically took priority over schooling, whether a child was taught at home or at school. Cows needed to be fed and milked; linens had to be marked; floors had to be swept; and chamber pots had to be emptied. In many instances these tasks could not wait, but book learning could.

In the 1700s and early 1800s, apprenticeships provided children with the opportunity to learn a trade. Apprenticeships were part of a centuries'-old tradition whereby a young child, usually a boy, would be contracted to a master craftsman (someone skilled in a trade and qualified to teach it to another). Frequently the apprenticeship was initiated by

INDENTURE FOR
HOUSEWIFERY

*Contract between appren-
tice Sarah Stout and mas-
ter Peter Sutter*

*Philadelphia, Pennsylvania;
1785*

*Col. 288 61 x 9.17 Downs
Collection, Winterthur
Library*

Children typically served
apprenticeships, during
which they learned a
trade, between the ages of
fourteen and twenty-one.
A formal contract spelled
out the terms of the
apprenticeship. Although
most apprentices were
boys, Sarah Stout entered
into this contract with
master Peter Sutter in
1785.

the child's father. A formal contract, or indenture, detailed the terms of the apprenticeship, often stipulating that the apprentice would live with the master. The master agreed to teach the child a trade or work skills as well as to provide a basic education and religious training. The contract specified a set period of time for the apprenticeship and frequently included a form of payment, often in the form of room and board, clothing, or tools. In return, a child promised to work hard and to lead a good life. The exact nature of the work performed varied depending on the trade involved as well as on the desires of the master. In learning the cabinetmaking trade, for example, a boy began by performing simple tasks, such as sweeping up the sawdust and debris in the workshop, chopping wood for the fire, and oiling the stones used to sharpen tools. By the second and third year, he would be entrusted with more complicated tasks, such as the steady rotation of the great wheel lathe while the master produced turnings for furniture legs and chair rails. Many contracts dictated that the apprentice not "haunt alehouses, Taverns, and Playhouses"; "commit fornication"; or "contract matrimony" during the term of the apprenticeship.

Although many apprenticeships were mutually agreed upon, others represented something closer to servitude or slavery because neither the parents nor the child entered into the agreement willingly. Orphans and children of the poor were frequently considered free labor to be worked long hours and fed as little as possible.

In the 1800s, children began to work in mills and factories. Factory jobs required much longer hours and provided less variety than working at home. As late as the 1850s, child labor in America was consid-

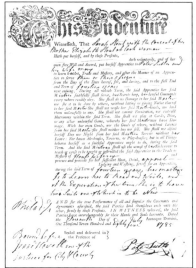

ered a social fact, not a social problem. Only later did reformers expose the often shameful conditions under which children worked and campaign for laws to prevent the use and abuse of child labor. Beginning in the 1840s, several northeastern states passed legislation regulating the number of hours per day a child would be allowed to work in a factory. In 1842, for example, Massachusetts and Connecticut adopted laws that limited the working day for children under twelve to ten hours. In 1848 Pennsylvania barred children under the age of twelve from working in a factory altogether. Although legislation sought to protect child workers, employers often found ways to circumvent the law, or the law was not enforced.

Between 1700 and 1900, parents took seriously their obligation to help their children learn the lessons necessary for leading a good life. Whether the lessons emphasized religious training or patriotic duty, parents strove to instill important moral values in their children. They appreciated the need for a child to be literate and to have the skills necessary to lead a fulfilling life. Parents of all economic classes knew the value of having a strong work ethic and possessing the necessary skills to be self-sufficient. A positive attitude toward work was considered as important as having good moral values and perhaps more important than being able to sign one's name.

PLAYTIME

NOAH'S ARK

Germany; 1880–1900

65.2107 Winterthur
Museum, bequest of Henry
Francis du Pont

Like adults in modern times, adults in early America appreciated the value of recreation, both for themselves and for their children. What has changed over time is the way in which adults structure playtime and the number and kinds of playthings available.

Before 1770 the concept of playtime was not applied exclusively to children. Adults and children enjoyed similar amusements, but recreation seldom involved specialized equipment. A family might play blindman's buff or tag; they might share card games or enjoy simple toys, such as dice or dominoes. Few child-specific toys existed in colonial America.

By the time of the Revolution, parents recognized the instructional benefits of play—it was a good way for children to exercise their bodies, develop their identities, and educate their minds. Many outdoor games helped develop hand-eye coordination, an important skill, as well as physical strength. Stimulating a child's imagination also gained greater attention, and while some toys were designed simply to entertain, others were developed to help teach children their adult roles. Playing

Lucky was the child who owned a toy Noah's ark. In his 1915 autobiography *A Child and a Boy,* Walter Brooks fondly recalled his childhood and the time spent playing with his prized plaything: "The Noah's ark helped me pass many a tedious day when minor floods were abroad and its hoards of paired inhabitants were an endless source of diversion and speculation."

DOLL

*Possibly Philadelphia,
Pennsylvania; 1835–45*

*91.23 Winterthur Museum,
gift of Ruth Young Buggy
in memory of Caroline
Bacon Willoughby Young*

Few mid nineteenth-century dolls survive in such good condition and with such documentation as "Mary Ann." A cotton doll with a jointed body, "Mary Ann" was lovingly and elaborately dressed by Harriet Bacon Slocum and her sisters to represent their mother, Mary Ann Warder Bacon. The shoes, corset, undergarments, and bonnet were all made by craftsmen who specialized in women's clothing. The doll became a cherished family possession, carefully handed down from generation to generation along with stories of the Bacon family.

with wooden farm animals prepared a boy for the day he would assume management of the family farm; dressing a doll helped a girl learn to care for the children she would eventually have.

Outdoor play, a necessity in colonial times, when houses were small and interior space limited, received new emphasis in the 1800s, when many children spent long hours working indoors at factory jobs. Parents encouraged children to play outdoors in the fresh air. Rolling hoops, skipping rope, riding a tricycle, and playing games such as marbles and battledore and shuttlecock (much like modern badminton) all promoted good health and physical development.

During this time, indoor play changed not so much in nature as in variety. In the 1800s, widespread industrialization made toys increasingly affordable to all economic levels of society. Toys to excite, toys to stimulate the senses, and toys to inspire wonder and awe became more widely available. Along with this proliferation of toys came an expanded notion of playtime as a time for recreation. Although they recognized the benefits of toys as aids in promoting physical and mental development, parents increasingly encouraged children to play "just for fun." Fanciful toys provided endless opportunities for creative play on rainy afternoons. Some toys chirped, whistled, or squeaked when squeezed. Others whirled, twirled, or hummed. A bird toy might even be made to peck. All of this movement and action delighted and amused children.

In early America, as today, many playthings were classified as boys' toys or girls' toys. Some child development specialists in the 1800s thought that children would be happier playing with toys deemed appropriate for their gender. Toys for boys generally involved outdoor play, made noise, or required strength to operate. Sporting equipment, toy soldiers, and riding toys all served the purpose. These toys taught boys their expected roles as adults and encouraged them to be strong and in control of any situation. Alternately, girls' playthings were often small and fragile and intended for quiet, indoor play. Girls' playthings included paper dolls, tea sets, and craft items, such as collage albums. These toys encouraged young ladies to develop delicate and genteel natures. Despite the claims of early child development specialists, however, children's diaries and reminiscences reveal that boys and girls often enjoyed playing with toys made for the opposite gender.

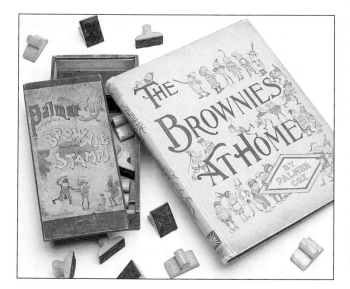

While a proliferation of children's toys and games emerged in the period between 1700 and 1900, many children never had more to play with than what they could fashion themselves from readily available materials: a string for the game of cat's cradle, a barrel hoop to be rolled as a hoop, a book made from scraps of wastepaper. Determination and imagination could turn the simplest object into a fanciful plaything. Certainly, some fortunate children possessed store-bought dolls, but others created dolls from the flower of a hollyhock or from rags. With acorns, a child could create a tea set as well equipped as the lucky child who owned a set of tiny porcelain dishes. Almost anything round could be used as a ball, and a stick made a perfectly fine bat. What survives, of course, are the special toys that families cherished and preserved, but diaries, letters, and images all testify to the existence of other, less exalted playthings.

What all children had, and still have, is a love of play. No matter how busy the day, no matter how many chores await, no matter how few material possessions a child has, playtime remains a vital activity that children always find time to explore.

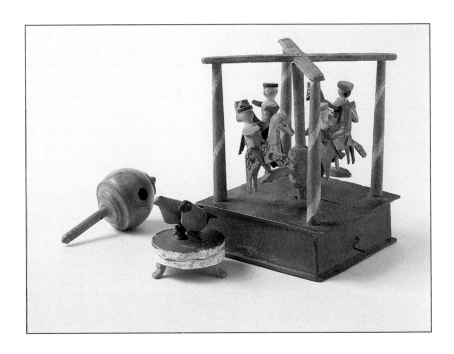

TOY SOLDIERS

Sold by B. Payn's Sons

Albany, New York;
1890–1920

Col. 121 80 x 243.4 Downs
Collection, Winterthur
Library

In the past as today, little boys (and not-so-little boys) loved lining up tin soldiers and marching them into battle. This creative play stimulated a child's imagination and introduced the male child to a world he might well inhabit one day, that of a soldier. Some nineteenth-century parents, however, believed that playing with toy soldiers glorified war, and, like some parents today, they actively discouraged such play.

MINIATURE DISHES

Staffordshire, England;
1825–40

59.1017.1–.42 Winterthur
Museum, gift of Henry
Francis du Pont

The abilities to set a fashionable table, serve a lavish meal, and host an elegant tea party were important skills for well-to-do women in early America. Girls practiced entertaining by playing with miniature tea, coffee, and dinner sets. It is unlikely, however, that the fortunate young girl who owned this set of dishes thought of such play as a rehearsal for adulthood. She probably simply enjoyed playing with the tiny dishes and pretending she was hosting a party.

200 YEARS OF CHILDHOOD

Over two centuries, from the early 1700s through the 1800s, adult perceptions of childhood evolved from the close integration of children within the adult world to the conscious separation of them from this same world. In the early 1700s, parents felt that the best way to protect children from the dangers of childhood was to guide them as quickly as possible to adulthood. They therefore made few changes to their homes to accommodate children, and few playthings or child-size furnishings existed. Instead, parents expected children to become part of the adult world. The use of walking stools and baby corsets hastened this transition from infancy to adulthood.

By the time of the American Revolution, new ideas about childhood emerged. Parents believed children were born into the world as a "tabula rasa," or blank slate. It fell to the parents or adults who raised a child to mold his or her character lovingly, to fill in that blank slate in order to produce an upright, moral, and literate child who would maintain these qualities into adulthood. This change in perspective resulted in

MIDDLE AGE: THE SEASON OF STRENGTH

From Wood, Struthers & Winthrop, Collection of Currier & Ives *(New York, 1996), pl. 6.*

Prints, portraits, and paintings of children during the late 1800s emphasized their innocent and pure nature. This lithograph depicts children as the focus of the family.

TIGERS

Probably Zanzibar;
1800–1870

56.38.84, .85 Winterthur
Museum

Play came to be seen as
an important activity for
children after the
American Revolution.
These toy tigers, made as
children's toys, were probably brought from Africa
by American merchants
and sea captains as sou-
venirs for their children.

the increased production of furniture forms crafted especially for children, in the development of educational children's books, and in the creation of toys designed to teach children their future roles. In addition, clothing became less restrictive to encourage a child's natural development.

In many ways, it is with these attitudes toward childhood that we can most closely identify today. In the mid-1700s, adults, influenced by Enlightenment philosophers, viewed childhood as a distinct and natural phase of human development, one that should be acknowledged and cherished instead of hastened or feared. Playtime offered an opportunity to improve a child's physical and mental well-being. Lightweight, nonrestrictive clothing; adult furniture forms sized for a child; and toys designed to instruct are all familiar items compatible with a modern view of childhood.

By contrast, parents in the 1800s viewed the adult world as a dangerous place and sought to protect children by isolating them from its corrupting influences. The addition of a nursery to many homes physically separated children from the adult world, and specialized equipment, such as high chairs and the increasing variety of children's toys, further differentiated a child's world from that of an adult. Clothing de-emphasized the physical differences between boys and girls, delaying recognition of sexuality and safeguarding their innocence.

For most children, however, this state of happy ignorance could not be prolonged indefinitely, for work was as much a part of a child's early world as play. Whether working on a farm or in a factory, children soon confronted